Tamasha Theatre Company

Artistic Directors: Sudha Bhuchar, Kristine Landon-Smith
General Manager: Kathy Bourne

'A major national Asian theatre company producing new writing theatre that draws from Asian literature and contemporary Asian life in Britain and abroad.'
London Arts Board

'A highly successful company of national importance, producing high quality Asian theatre, that is visual, powerful and thought provoking.'
The Arts Council of England

Kristine Landon-Smith and Sudha Bhuchar formed Tamasha in 1989 to adapt *Untouchable* a classic Indian novel by Mulk Raj Anand. After an extremely successful debut the company has gone from strength to strength. Tamasha aims to reflect through theatre the Asian experience – from British Asian life to authentic accounts of life in the Indian sub-continent, adapting works of literature and classics to commissioning new work from a range of contemporary writers.

Tamasha Theatre Company, 11 Ronalds Road, London N5 1XJ

Tel. 0171 609 2411   *Fax.* 0171 609 2722
E-mail: general@tamasha.demon.co.uk
Website: http//www.tamasha.demon.co.uk

With the Compliments of

THE NOON FOUNDATION (U.K.)

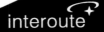

A YEARNING

A Yearning was co-produced with Birmingham Repertory
Theatre and first performed at their Studio Theatre on
26 September 1995 with the following cast:

JAZ	Riz Abbasi
AMAR, his wife	Sudha Bhuchar
ARVIND, her cousin	Faroque Khan
MEDIUM, GOSSIP, WOMAN AT FESTIVAL	Surendra Kochar
DARSHANA, GOSSIP	Archie Panjabi
BACHAN, GOSSIP, SISTER-IN-LAW, GIRL	Zita Sattar
OLD LADY, GOSSIP	Zohra Segal
MEETA, GOSSIP, SISTER-IN-LAW, YOUNG GIRL	Harvey Virdi

Director Kristine Landon-Smith
Designer Sue Mayes
Lighting Designer Paul Taylor
Composer and Musical Director Ansuman Biswas
Literal translation Gwenda Pandolfi
Sound Designer Mike Furness

ACT ONE

Scene 1

Birmingham. Day. AMAR *is sleeping on a settee facing a TV set on which a Hindi video movie plays. A sewing machine with sari material has been abandoned. The music dissolves into the sound of a baby crying. It becomes unnaturally loud.* AMAR *is smiling in her dream.* JAZ, AMAR's *husband enters, shirtless and shaving. He sees she is asleep and switches off TV. He then exits.* AMAR *wakes.*

AMAR. Jaz? Is that you?

JAZ (*offstage*). Yea, yea. I'm up.

AMAR. Did you rest?

JAZ (*entering*). Not bad. You left the video on. It wears out the heads.

AMAR (*affectionate*). Come here.

JAZ. Amar, I've got to go to work. Vaisakhi, a busy time. Those boys, you can't afford to let a fly rest on your nose and they are fiddling the books.

As JAZ *puts on his shoes* AMAR *begins to massage his neck and shoulders.*

AMAR. Did you drink some milk?

JAZ. I'm not thirsty.

AMAR. An egg, let me cook you an egg.

JAZ. I'll eat later. Got to push off.

AMAR. You work too hard. That's why you're getting thin.

JAZ. I prefer to be slim. Slimmer is healthier. Stronger.

AMAR. You're too thin!

JAZ. I've always been slim.

AMAR. No. In your picture your face was fuller.

JAZ. In my picture! It was a terrible photograph. Made me look like an owl.

AMAR. It's a beautiful photograph. Your face was full. Chubby. Healthy.

JAZ. That was puppy fat.

AMAR. Now your skin is like ash. Like it's been hiding from the sun.

JAZ pulls away from her to put on his leather jacket and assemble his keys, documents. He checks his mobile phone.

JAZ. Night worker, aren't I? What do you expect? Sunburn?

AMAR. Jaz, we've been married twenty-four months and each month I see you getting sadder and sadder, thinner and thinner, as if you were growing backwards.

JAZ. Thanks!

AMAR. Don't take it the wrong way! Jaz, please. All I meant was – if I were ill, you'd be the same, you'd worry about me, you'd find ways to make me better. You would search out a healer. 'My wife is sick, give me your best medicine, your best advice.' You'd buy me the freshest foods, the tenderest meat . . . That's the way I am. That's why I take care of you! Don't you see?

JAZ. Yea. Yea. And I'm grateful. All right. Only I've got to push off.

AMAR (*on the point of tears*). But you won't let me take care of you.

JAZ sighs, puts his arm around her.

JAZ. Because there is nothing wrong with me! (*Smiles at her affectionately.*) It's all in your mind, baby. It is all in your mind. I work hard. Each year I get older. It's a law of nature.

AMAR. A law of nature . . .

JAZ. It's tough out there. Tougher than Glasgow. Competitive. Next year maybe I can take on another cab. Luckily we don't have children to lay out on.

AMAR suddenly holds on to him tightly.

AMAR. Oh Jaz!

JAZ. What is it with you?

AMAR. You know I love you.

JAZ (*he's said it many times before*). I know you love me.

AMAR. You know I love you properly.

JAZ. You love me properly.

AMAR. Some girls tremble and cry on their wedding night. One girl in my village, they had to give her drugs.

JAZ *disengages himself.*

But I wasn't like that. I didn't weep. I was smiling, wasn't I? I was smiling. And wasn't I singing when I turned back the wedding sheets? And didn't I say to you, 'The sheets smell of spring rain? Of spring rain'?

JAZ. That's what you said.

AMAR. My mother cried and cried because I wasn't sad to be leaving her. I wasn't. I was so happy. I looked all the time at the photograph of you and I couldn't wait. No girl in the world was happier than me to be married. Even if it meant leaving the warmth and sun of my village, the bright colours, I was happy. (*She starts to weep.*) I was happy.

JAZ. Oh for God's sake. Be quiet. It's enough, too much, the things I'm having to hear –

AMAR No, no, don't. (*Her hands over her ears.*) I don't want to know what people are saying. It's not true, whatever they're saying. They can think and say what they like, but I KNOW, in my village there are flowers that only come every other year, every five years, ten years, depending on the rain. Depending on the rain.

JAZ (*placating*). We've got to be patient.

AMAR. Yes. And love each other as much as we can.

A ring on his mobile phone.

JAZ (*he really has to go. Of videos:*). I'll get you a couple of new ones.

AMAR. I can get them myself.

JAZ. You know I don't like you out of doors on your own. The streets are dangerous. Women get raped, faces slashed. I don't want you out on your own. You need anything, just say so, I'll get it for you. Lock the doors and rest and I'll see you in the morning. All right?

AMAR (*gloomily*). All right.

JAZ leaves and AMAR *is alone. She bolts and locks the doors after him. She dims a light unplaits her hair, stretches, raises her arms, strokes her belly as she sings to it. The song begins in Punjabi and melts into English.*

From where do you come, my love, my child?
From where do you come?

(*Musically child's voice.*)

'From the cold, far away, far away
From the high blue cold.'

What do you need, my love my child?
What do you need, when your time is come?

'To be warmed by the curve of your arm, the whisper of your breath, the fullness of your breast.'

Let the branches of the trees wave to the sun! The warm
    rains fall!
Let my arms be soft to hold you
Let my breath be sweet
Let my breasts be full.
To welcome you, my child.

(*As if speaking to a child.*)

Whatever you need is here for you.
Whatever you ask shall be given for you
Let the branches of the trees wave to the sun! The warm
    rains fall!
When, my child will you come?
I'm broken in for you
Inside me a cradle awaits you
My womb, aching for you
When, my child, will you come?

AMAR *exits. Fade to dark. Fade up. It is morning.* AMAR *working the sewing machine. She is in a happy mood. She has spotted someone outside the window and raps on it. She unbolts the door to beckon in* DARSHNA, *a young woman carrying a large shopping bag.*

AMAR. Come in, Darshna, come in. It's so nice to see you. You're looking well.

DARSHNA. Yes. How are you Amar?

AMAR. I'm – the same. Let me get you a drink, something to eat.

DARSHNA. I have to get back or my mother-in-law will be having one of her turns. You're lucky in a way. Just you and Jaz. All to yourselves.

AMAR (*melancholy*). All to ourselves. (*Attempting to brighten up.*) You've been shopping. Something nice?

DARSHNA (*excited*). You'll never guess.

AMAR. Not MORE shoes!

DARSHNA. It finally happened.

AMAR. What?

DARSHNA *opens the bags to show her: a set of baby clothes and a rattle. Baby knitting wool.*

AMAR. In five months! That's wonderful! You're sure?

DARSHNA. Absolutely positive.

AMAR. It's so wonderful. How does it feel?

DARSHNA. I don't know. Different. A bit odd. Like I can't quite believe it.

AMAR (*holding on to her*). Different? How? Darshna, tell me, the night it happened, were you carried away – did you cry out with happiness that time? The moment when it happened did you know immediately, or has it come as a complete surprise?

DARSHNA. I suppose it was a bit of a surprise. And yet at the time . . . I did feel . . . I don't know Amar. I'm just so glad it's happened for me.

AMAR. I expect it WAS different that night.

DARSHNA. Don't go on about it Amar. It's embarrassing.

AMAR. Sorry, I just – (*She can't complete the sentence.*)

DARSHNA (*taking pity*). Look, have you ever held a live bird shut in your hand?

AMAR. Yes. When I was in my village we caught birds.

DARSHNA. Well it's the same, but in your blood.

AMAR. How beautiful!

DARSHNA. I'm still in a daze about it all. You know me, Amar, bags of confidence, but as soon as it was confirmed, I realised I don't know anything about births or babies. I'll have to talk to my Mum.

AMAR. Of course, you know! It's a natural thing. Your body was made for you to have a child. *It* knows. Just be sure you don't rush around too much and when you breathe, breathe as softly as if you had a flower between your teeth.

DARSHNA. 'Flower between my teeth?' Where d'you get that one from!

AMAR. I've heard my aunties in my village. It's all they talk about. Babies and husbands. You pick it up. That's how you learn at home. Listening in on the wise women.

DARSHNA. They say later on it starts kicking you, pushing you to get out.

AMAR. Yes, and that's when you love it the most, when you can really call him, 'my child'. It's a good sign. He's feeling his way inside you. Getting to know you.

DARSHNA. Amar!

AMAR (*shyly*). Darshna what did Manjit say when you told him?

DARSHNA. Nothing much. (*Smiles.*) Grunted a bit. You know what he's like. He's not a talker.

AMAR. But he loves you very deeply, doesn't he?

DARSHNA. I suppose so. Yea. I suppose he does. Doesn't put it into words like, but when he lies real close to me, you know, his eyes they quiver like two leaves in a breeze.

AMAR. The moment it happened, d'you think he knew?

DARSHNA. He could tell.

AMAR. He knew?

DARSHNA. On our wedding night he kept saying it, repeating it over and over 'come on baby, come on baby', over and over, his mouth pressed against my cheek 'come on' so that now I think of my baby like something he slipped into my ear. But you're the expert, Amar, you know more about these things than I do. Than most of us do.

AMAR. Much good it does me! You are so lucky Darshna! So lucky.

DARSHNA. Doesn't seem fair. Of all the girls who got married when you did, you're the only one –

AMAR (cutting in). That's how it is. And there's plenty of time. It took Kiran three years and in the village there was a woman who had to wait *twelve* years before it happened. But you're quite right, two years and twenty days is too long for me to wait. Eaten up with longing, counting each day, waiting each month. Inside me, I'm wasting away. It isn't fair. I dare not tell Jaz, but sometimes I feel so bad I go to the park just to press my back against a tree, to feel it growing. If I go on like this, I'll go mad.

DARSHNA. Amar, you've got to stop carrying on in this way. You're sounding like a demented old woman. Moaning on isn't going to help, is it? One of my mother's sisters had a baby when she was forty! He came out perfect, lovely looking baby as well. And so healthy.

AMAR. Was he?

DARSHNA. He was a terror. Made a noise like six Bhangra dancers in competition with a heavy metal band. He used to pee on us all and pull our plaits and when he was just four months old he used to scratch our faces. They were quite sharp those nails of his. Little tiger, he was and really strong.

AMAR (laughing). But he was a baby. Babies can't really hurt.

DARSHNA. You reckon!

AMAR. My eldest sister when she was feeding her first baby I remember her breasts were covered with scratches, cracked and sore and it really hurt her, but it was a good pain, healthy. The old women in the village said it was a wholesome pain.

DARSHNA. Well my sister, the one who's married to the councillor, she's got four and she reckons children bring you pain, wrinkles, thick hips and aggravation.

AMAR. Of course you have to suffer, but nobody said having a child is like arranging a bunch of flowers! Why have them if you're not prepared to suffer to see them grow. It is said we lose our blood to make a child. So we must suffer. But that is good, healthy, beautiful. Every woman is made with enough blood for four or five children and if it's not used her blood turns to poison. As mine will.

DARSHNA Amar!

AMAR. Sorry, sorry, sorry, this is your happy day.

DARSHNA. Oh God Amar I feel so strange. As if my body isn't mine.

AMAR (*practical, sensible mode*). It is always said: the first is the worst but also the most treasured.

DARSHNA. Yea?

DARSHNA *unwraps skeins of blue wool.*

Amar, you're clever with your hands.

AMAR (*taking the wool, holding it to her face*). So soft, give it here. I have a lovely pattern. I'll make a beautiful shawl for your beautiful baby. I'd love to.

DARSHNA. You're so good Amar. I'll see you later.

She goes over to AMAR *who cups her hands lovingly round* DARSHNA's *belly.*

AMAR. Take it easy. Don't run.

They kiss goodbye.

DARSHNA. And don't worry Amar, one day it will happen for you. (*Punjabi.*) Goodbye.

AMAR (*Punjabi*). Goodbye. Visit me again soon.

DARSHNA *leaves.*

AMAR *holding the baby wool close to her face, opens the back door to breathe in the sunlight.*

She begins knitting. She sings the first, second and last verse of 'From where will you come my child' which melts into Punjabi. Over this ARVIND (*her male cousin*) *enters to drop in banking books/accounts.*

AMAR Arvind!

ARVIND. Who was the door open for?

AMAR. For the air, for the sun, for life!

ARVIND. Jaz around?

AMAR. Still working.

ARVIND (*of wool*). What are you making?

AMAR. A little shawl and if there is enough left an embroidered bonnet to go with it.

ARVIND (*smiling*). Well, well!

AMAR. I might sew lace all round the edges.

ARVIND. And if it is a girl, she'll take your name?

AMAR. What.. . what are you saying?

ARVIND. Amar, I'm very happy for you. Congratulations.

AMAR (*shocked*). No . . . it's not for me, not for my baby. It's for Darshna. Darshna is expecting a child.

ARVIND (*uncomfortable, having put his foot in it*). Maybe you'll be following her example. This house needs a child. Sarbjit Kaur is always writing from home 'When is your cousin having her child? . . . tell her (*Clowning using stage Indian to lighten the mood.*) in the conception department melon is very fortifying for ladies. Give your cousin melons, ginger, tell her to put a tikka behind *both* ears.'

AMAR *tries to laugh.*

And tell that husband of yours (ARVIND *using this mimicry to put over his thoughts too.*) to think less about work, tell him to dig deeper!

AMAR. Yes. Dig deeper.

ARVIND (*levelling*). Jaz works too hard. What is he wanting to make all his money *for*? Who does he intend to leave it to when he dies? There are no Barclays Banks in the next life. (*He places account books on shelves. Leaving.*) Tell Jaz the brakes on the Honda are dodgy. And take care, eh?

AMAR (*to herself*). Deeper! Much deeper! (*Sings.*)
'My child, it's true
I'm torn and broken in for you.
My womb an empty cradle aches for you,
When, my child, when will you come. (*Repeat in Punjabi.*)

She moves to the spot where ARVIND *stood and breathes in deeply as if inhaling sea air. She then searches in the room for a box (under drapes). Its shape and size reminds us of a child's coffin. In her search for lace for the shawl she takes out baby clothes wrapped in paper. She replaces them carefully and sits on the settee to knit. She manages a few stitches and then becomes abstracted, staring unfocused at one spot.*

Scene Two

Some months later: we note a change in AMAR, *externally less exuberant, more contained, but inside her rage at her condition has intensified. In a park. City litter.* AMAR *with Tesco bags sits on a bench throwing crumbs to birds. An* OLD WOMAN *shuffles with her shopping bag, sees* AMAR *and eases herself beside her.*

AMAR. Saat Sri Akaal.

OLD WOMAN. Saat Sri Akaal. And how are you?

AMAR. It's a beautiful day.

OLD WOMAN. You call this beautiful!

AMAR. The sky isn't angry.

OLD WOMAN (*of* AMAR's *bags*). You've been shopping.

AMAR. My husband usually does it, but business is taking him to the airport this week.

OLD WOMAN. He is a porter?

AMAR. No, he has his own business. Mini cabs.

OLD WOMAN. Very nice. Have you been married long?

AMAR. Three years, and twenty days.

OLD WOMAN. How many children?

AMAR None.

OLD WOMAN. Bah! They will come.

AMAR (*cynical note*). Do you really think so?

OLD WOMAN. Why not. I've just been shopping too. Boots
talcum powder three for the price of two today. Tesco cheap
apricots, but not ripe. And they will not ripen. Picked too
early. Buy them, and they will go bad in your fruit bowl.
My husband he likes his apricots. He is old but still working.
I've got nine children.

AMAR. Nine!

OLD WOMAN. Like nine shining suns they are, but there is not
a single girl among them, so here I am always running from
one place to the other to be fair to all my grandchildren. And
now I have to catch my bus.

AMAR. You live on the South side?

OLD WOMAN By the old warehouses. Who is your family?

AMAR. At home in my village my people have land. Some are
farmers.

OLD WOMAN. In your village, it's another world. Here, who is
your connection here?

AMAR My cousin Arvind, he came over when he was fifteen.
My husband was born here.

OLD WOMAN. You came as a bride, yes? I can tell! Your
husband's family name?

AMAR. Talwar.

OLD WOMAN. 'Talwar.' I know this family. (*She makes a
comically sombre face.*) Good people. Get up, work hard, eat
some roti and die! Silent creatures, no smiles, no laughter, no

fun and games. I could have married one of your husband's uncles. I didn't want him. I've always been a woman who must have laughter. Laughter and music. Otherwise I might as well be a cracked jug. Any Bhangra dancing I'm there – my heart singing. The music stays in my head for days. I get up in the deep of the night convinced I can hear the Bhangra drums approaching. I open the window but it's only the bloody miserable English wind crying to be let in.

She glances at AMAR, *introspective. She nudges her.*

This will make you laugh. I've had two husbands, fourteen children, five of them died and yet I refuse to be sad. I've still got a lot of life in me yet. My mother used to say: 'Look how long neem trees last! How long houses stand! It's only us poor women who crumble away to dust at the slightest thing.'

AMAR. Can I ask you something?

OLD WOMAN (*looking at* AMAR *and nodding*). My dear I already know what it is you're going to say. (*She gets up.*) Such things are best left unasked.

AMAR (*detaining her*). Please. Why not? I can speak freely with an older woman. I can tell you know things. Please, I must find out –

OLD WOMAN. What? What is it you MUST find out?

AMAR (*low, intense*). Tell me, why am I like a barren desert inside? Why am I meant to spend my fruitful years feeding birds that are fat! Putting up net curtains where no one looks, dusting where there is no dust! Tell me what I should do to have a child, whatever it is, I'll do it, even if I have to stick needles into my eyes, I will do it, tell me!

OLD WOMAN. What can I tell you? All I did was to lie on my back and sing and smile. Children came like rain. (*Deliberately coded.*) All I can say to you: You have a beautiful young body. Even I can see that and my eyes are failing. When you step out doesn't the mangiest dog in the street start sniffing. That's so isn't it?

AMAR (*totally puzzled*). Dog? What dog?

OLD WOMAN. Oh for goodness sake!

AMAR. But what, please –

18

OLD WOMAN. Don't make me talk. Some matters better not to say.

AMAR. But why not? I talk to my husband about it all the time.

OLD WOMAN (*pause*). Tell me something: this husband of yours. Do you love him? Do you yearn for him when he is not there?

AMAR. Yearn for him? I don't know.

OLD WOMAN. When he comes close to you, do you tremble? When his lips touch you, are you not carried away so that it all seems a wonderful dream?

AMAR. No, I've never felt that. No. I haven't ever felt like that.

OLD WOMAN. Never? Not even when you have been dancing?

AMAR (*recalling*). Once – in my village, my cousin Arvind . . .

OLD WOMAN. Go on.

AMAR. I was about twelve, just before he left for this country, my cousin Arvind . . . musicians came to the village. We were all dancing . . . something happened. I tripped and fell. He held my hands to pull me up. I couldn't speak. I was trembling, but not because I had fallen, because – but I've always been shy.

OLD WOMAN. And how is it when your husband touches you?

AMAR. A husband. It's different. My father chose him for me. And I accepted, straight away. Gladly. That's the honest truth. And from the very day it was arranged, even before I came here, I was already thinking of the children we would have together. And when we met and I looked at my reflection in his eyes I saw myself very small, very obedient, as if I was my own daughter.

OLD WOMAN. The very exact opposite of me. Maybe this is the reason you have not yet made a child. Our men must give us pleasure, unplait our hair, fondle us into the right mood, prepare us for their seed, they must make us feel like a flower thirsting for rain . . . A man's hunger and a woman's thirst, that is what makes the world go round.

AMAR. I have so many dreams of a son. And the life he will have. I see him growing into a wonderful man. It is for his sake that I give myself to my husband, to make my son, but never for my own pleasure.

OLD WOMAN. And the result is: you're empty.

AMAR. No, not empty. Because I'm filling up with hate. Hate and rage. Tell me the truth, is it wrong of me to want a man not just for himself? Because in that case what are you to think of when he turns over on his side to sleep while you lie there staring sadly at the dark? Am I to fill my mind with thoughts of just him or about the miracle of creation that may be happening inside me? Once the seed is planted do you dream of the seedling or the husk?

She clasps the OLD WOMAN'S *hand.*

Tell me, am I wrong to feel like this? Because I don't know any more.

OLD WOMAN. You know, but you don't want to know that you know! You are a flower in bloom. A beautiful creature. Don't make me say more.

AMAR *holds on to the* OLD WOMAN.

These are matters of honour and I don't destroy people's honour. You'll find out everything for yourself. But try to grow up. You are so beautiful, but so intense. Now, I've said enough.

AMAR. I don't know what it is you're saying to me. I can't understand anything any more because everything here is a smudge of hints and nudges and nobody will be direct. There is no real kindness. Behind the sun there is always cold.

The OLD WOMAN *pats* AMAR *to calm and quieten her.*

When I talk about my problem, I am told it is not a problem to talk about. You, you're just the same. You carry on as if you know everything but when I press, no, you refuse to share with me your wisdom and the knowledge I'm dying of thirst for. It's cruel.

OLD WOMAN. I could advise another woman, a woman who was calmer, I could give her plenty of advice. But not to you! I'm old enough to know what I am doing.

AMAR. Then God help me!

She releases the OLD WOMAN'*s hand.*

OLD WOMAN It's not God you must cry out to! What if he doesn't exist. To whom do you turn? And when are you going to realise that the help you seek is not just for yourself?

AMAR. What are you telling me?

OLD WOMAN (*leaving*). I don't myself care for Gods, but there should be one, if only a little one to deal with men whose rotten seed brings nothing but tears!

AMAR. I don't understand what it is you are saying!

OLD WOMAN. Well I do. And I'm advising you: Don't be so sad. Keep dreaming. Keep hoping. You are still young. What more are you expecting me to say?

AMAR *picks up her shopping and exits.*

OLD WOMAN (*to audience/herself*). Those who can dream can sleep. Those who can sleep cannot always dream.

The same day. AMAR'*s house.* AMAR *working her sewing machine (making a silken suit). There is a buzz on the door and she lets in* MEETA *and* BACHAN. *The suit* AMAR *is making is for* MEETA.

MEETA. Just popped in to see if it's ready.

AMAR. I'm sorry, I got held up.

AMAR *unfolds the dress she has made for* BACHAN *and gives it to her to try on.* BACHAN *goes behind screen to change into it.*

MEETA. That's all right Amar. I'll pop back another time. I was on my way to the chemist, got some Ribena. Cost a fortune the way he goes through it. Better hurry in case he wakes.

AMAR. Meeta, you left your child alone in the house?

MEETA It's all right he is sleeping.

AMAR. You can't leave a small child alone, accidents can happen. The slightest fall, a little child can DROWN in three inches of water!

MEETA. He's in his cot!

BACHAN *appears in the dress.*

AMAR. He could suffocate!

MEETA (*making a face to* BACHAN *to suggest 'here she goes again' as she exits*). I'm going, I'm going, I'm going!

AMAR *works on fitting the dress for* BACHAN *– pinning hem, marking button holes etc: over this.*

AMAR. How could she do it? A little child all alone!

BACHAN. If you had four or five, maybe you would talk differently.

AMAR. Never. Even if I had forty!

BACHAN. You and me we don't have children, we don't have such problems. We have a quieter life.

AMAR. I don't have a quiet life.

BACHAN. Well I do and I like it. Except my mother is always pressing on me some concoction or other: herbs, ointments, some of them really stink! In April she's dragging me off to this new Guru that's supposed to make it happen for you. You have to kneel down and beg him. My mother can do the begging if she likes. I'm not.

AMAR. Bachan, why did you get married?

BACHAN. It was arranged for me. Everybody gets married in my family. Not allowed to be single. Mind you nowadays a lot of girls get married before their wedding day. It's the old fashioned people we have to get married for. Ouch!

A pin has pricked her hand.

AMAR. Sorry.

BACHAN. I'm nineteen, right? And I hate housework, food shopping, having to visit all those boring relatives every weekend . . . I'm spending my life doing things that don't interest me in the slightest. What for? Why is it necessary for my husband to be my husband? We had a good time together before we were married. It's all crap. No one really believes in it anymore.

AMAR. Don't say that!

BACHAN. They all say I'm crazy. The crazy one in the family. Crazy Bachan! (*Laughs.*) One thing I notice since I've been

married: everybody is stuck in their houses doing things they
don't like. Being women they don't want to be. Cooking
samosas and watching videos. I want to go out, have a bit of
a rave, a few drinks with my friends, have a laugh. Not be
setting the table every night. Clearing the table. Taking the
dishes out. Putting the washing on. Putting it out. Bringing it
in. Oh God! I can't stand it!

AMAR. You're only a child.

BACHAN. But I'm not crazy.

AMAR. Bachan, your mother, she's a medium, isn't she?

BACHAN. She's a poser. They all pretend they have these spells
and things. It's a way old people try and have some power
over you. Her spells don't work any better than you going up
the clinic and having a torch being shined up you. If it's your
fate, it's your fate.

BACHAN *goes behind screen to change back into her*
clothes.

Where is it your mother lives Bachan?

She wipes a tear from her eye. And now she can't stop crying.
BACHAN *has changed and goes over to the weeping*
AMAR.

BACHAN (*tender*). There's more to life than babies, Amar –
don't cry. Don't cry, please don't cry . . .

BACHAN *tries to comfort* AMAR *but doesn't know how to*
do it. She leaves. AMAR *sits on settee, her head in her hands*
and then snatches a coat and leaves hurriedly.

Night. A street – outside the cab office. AMAR *approaches*
and hears ARVIND *singing from inside.*

ARVIND (*singing*). Why do you sleep alone, Man?
Why do you wake alone?
My bed is soft and warm
I can stretch out alone.

AMAR *is listening in the shadows. She joins in (quietly) in*
the song.

AMAR. Why do you sleep alone, Man?
Why do you wake alone?

My bed is soft and warm
I can stretch out alone

ARVIND. Sleep is not what I want
My bed is a desert without a woman to hold
Lost in a desert thirsting for water
Without a woman to hold
Better rocks and cold
Than a bed soft and empty

ARVIND *comes out of the office and spots* AMAR.

ARVIND. Hello Pet. Where are you off to?

AMAR. I didn't know you could sing like that. It was wonderful!

ARVIND. Thanks, I enjoy singing. I'm always singing to myself.

AMAR. Your voice, it's so (*Searching for the word.*) powerful – and so full of . . . happiness.

ARVIND. Well, I'm a cheerful person.

AMAR. Yes, you are. Always happy.

ARVIND. And you are always sad, right?

AMAR. I haven't always been sad, have I? There is a reason for my sadness. I wasn't born that way.

ARVIND. And your husband is even sadder than you are.

AMAR. He is, yes. He has a dry nature.

ARVIND. He's dry all right. Always been the same. Poor Jaz. It's like it costs him blood to laugh.

AMAR (*looking closely*). What's that?

She points to his face.

ARVIND. What?

AMAR. Here . . . (*Going over.*) on your cheek. A scratch.

ARVIND. It's nothing.

AMAR. As if a nail . . .

ARVIND. I must have done it shaving . . .

A beat. She realises her hand is still on his cheek. She drops it. He doesn't move. The silence between them intensifies. The tension of attraction between them is there unspoken.

AMAR (*whispering*). Did you hear it?

ARVIND. What?

AMAR. Can't you hear crying?

ARVIND (*listening*). No.

AMAR. I thought I heard a child crying.

ARVIND. Yea?

AMAR. Close by. A muffled sort of crying.

ARVIND. There are always kids around here. Mucking about.

AMAR. No. This is a baby crying.

ARVIND. I can't hear anything.

AMAR. It must be my imagination.

She looks directly at ARVIND *with a mesmerised expression. He returns her look for a beat. And then, as if afraid, turns away. A strong emotion has held them.* JAZ *enters with beer.*

JAZ (*to* AMAR). What are you doing still here? Didn't I tell you to stay in the house?

ARVIND. Bye. See you tomorrow.

AMAR. I stayed in the house.

JAZ (*to* AMAR). So what are you doing here?

AMAR. I needed air.

JAZ. You want people to gossip about you? To say bad things?

AMAR. To say things about me?

JAZ. I'm not talking about you. I'm talking about other people.

AMAR. Other people! Damn other people!

JAZ. Don't swear. It's not nice in a woman.

AMAR. I wish I were a woman!

JAZ. Come on. I'm not listening to this any more. I'm going to put you in a cab to take you home.

AMAR (*bitter*). Oh yes. And when will YOU be home?

JAZ (*angry*). When I have finished my business.

JAZ. It's late. I want you to go home and sleep.

AMAR (*ironic*). Sleep! Just like that.

> JAZ *leads* AMAR *out.*

> *End of Act One.*

ACT TWO

Scene One

The THIRD WOMAN's *house. The* WOMEN *come on singing.*

Pity the poor barren wife,
Pity the wife whose breasts are full of sand!

Tell me whether your man
Stores well his seed
So the waters will sing
in your billowing skirts.
Your skirt is a many sailed boat
A boat of silver in the breeze
Coasting along a welcoming shore.
My baby's shawl is ready to hold
The baby promising to unfold.

FIRST WOMAN. I don't like this gossiping.

THIRD WOMAN. Everyone gossips here.

FOURTH WOMAN. What harm is there in it?

FIFTH WOMAN. A woman who values her reputation makes
certain there is nothing for anyone to gossip about.

FOURTH WOMAN. A fire does not light itself.

FIFTH WOMAN. A tap does not turn itself on.

FIRST WOMAN. But it's all rumours, nothing but rumours.

FOURTH WOMAN. Her husband has brought his two sisters to
live with them. This is a fact, not a rumour.

FIFTH WOMAN. The old maids?

FOURTH WOMAN. They used to be in charge of attending to
the temple and now they're in charge of attending to sister in
law! I couldn't live with those two.

FIRST WOMAN. Why ever not? They are quiet enough. (*With
point.*) Not like some round here, yak, yak yak.

FOURTH WOMAN. They give you the creeps. They're quiet all right, like those dark plants that grow in the shade, with spikes on their leaves, not even a dog will pee on them.

THIRD WOMAN. And already they are in the house?

FOURTH WOMAN. Since last month. Now the husband can go to his business again.

FIRST WOMAN. Does anybody know exactly what happened?

FIFTH WOMAN. The night before last she was found outside the house. By herself. Nobody with her. Sitting outside the house all night. In the dark.

FIRST WOMAN. What was the reason?

FOURTH WOMAN. She cannot be inside her own house. All the time now she is running out.

FIFTH WOMAN. Typical. Manly women like that, it's how they carry on. When they should be attending to their husband's needs, cleaning and cooking, making the home cheerful and nice, they'd rather be walking in the streets, roaming in the parks. Once she was seen paddling barefoot in the children's pool, splashing the water like a little girl.

FIRST WOMAN. Why are you saying such cruel things? It's not her fault she doesn't have children.

FOURTH WOMAN. A woman who wants children, she has them. Yes, she finds a way. Too many girls now, they want all the luxuries a man can give them, but they don't want to spoil their beautiful bellies with stretch marks. And who but their husbands will be looking at their bellies anyway!

Laughter.

THIRD WOMAN. And they paint themselves up with garish colours, puff up their hair and wiggle their behinds and go looking for another man. Too many girls now like that.

FIRST WOMAN. But not one of us has seen her with another man.

FOURTH WOMAN. Maybe none of us, but other people have seen it.

FIRST WOMAN. Always other people!

FOURTH WOMAN. Twice now, she's been seen.

SECOND WOMAN. And what were they doing?

FOURTH WOMAN. Talking.

FIRST WOMAN. Now talking is a sin.

FOURTH WOMAN. There's a way of talking and there's a way of looking. A woman looking at roses has a very different look in her eye than a woman looking at a man's haunches. And she was looking at him like that. In that way.

FIRST WOMAN. At who? At who was she looking 'like that, in that way'?

FOURTH WOMAN. Someone. Use you head. Do you want me to shout it out in the streets, or maybe I should place an ad in the Birmingham Post (*Or Punjabi paper or radio station.*)

Laughter.

I'll tell you this, even when she is on her own and he is not there she carries his picture in her eyes. She sees him all the time!

FIRST WOMAN. You can't know that! I can't stand to listen to this.

She moves away from the group.

FIFTH WOMAN. And her husband?

THIRD WOMAN. Him! You'd think he was deaf, not a move – like a lizard in the sun!

Laughter.

FIRST WOMAN. It would all be sorted if they had children.

SECOND WOMAN. It's what comes from not accepting your kismet.

FOURTH WOMAN. The misery in that house increases with each hour. All day long she and her sisters in law without once opening their mouths, except to eat, are polishing the brass, cleaning the carpets, washing and sponging, dusting the ceiling even. But the cleaner that house, the more it shines, the hotter the flames inside.

FIRST WOMAN. It could be his fault too! When a man doesn't give his wife children he ought to pay her more attention.

FOURTH WOMAN. It's her fault. She's got a very sharp blade for a tongue.

FIRST WOMAN. Who are you to talk like this about another woman? What business is it of yours what happens between people who are not even your relatives?

FOURTH WOMAN. You are not so pure, you are one of these women who enjoys gossip and then mews 'we shouldn't really be saying these unkind things'.

SECOND WOMAN. Stop it, you two.

FIRST WOMAN. The only way to stop some slanderers is to skewer their tongues like a kebab!

FOURTH WOMAN. The tongues of hypocrites should be made to lick shit!

SECOND WOMAN. Stop it, now! (*Looking out of window.*) Cool down. We shouldn't be falling out over an unfortunate. It will bring us bad luck.

She begins to sing. The other WOMEN *join in.*

My husband at my table enjoys
The food and drink I make for him
He brings me a rose
And I bring him three
My husband breaks wood
And lights a fire
I breathe on it
to make it glow
My husband is ready to sleep
I'm a beautiful red rose
And he is rosy red and beautiful
Flowers intertwine with flowers
Summer saps the reaper's blood
Our limbs open to sleepless birds
Winter shivers at our doors.
We must moan between the sheets!
And we must sing!
Our man brings us flowers and fruits
Our arms are intertwined,

The stems of our branches quicken with life
And the winds howl to be let in
So that a child may melt
The Dawns spiky splinters
And our body holds in
The life that begins
A new life, a child.
And the birds open their wings and cry!
A new noisy baby, a son!
Let her shine, let her run,
Let her run again,
Let her sing,
Let her hide and let her sing again.

Evening: AMAR'*s house. The* TWO SISTERS *stand waiting.*
JAZ *seated, eating snacks, waiting.*

JAZ. You say she's out?

The SISTERS *nod.*

You know very well I don't like her being out alone.

Pause.

All right. You can lay the table.

The YOUNGER SISTER *leaves.*

JAZ. I work hard. I was driving all day, hardly a break, the
traffic and fumes they are killing me. And now my shoulders
– like there's a knife between them. All day working and I'm
thinking to myself 'what's the use to work so hard? So long?'
I haven't time to eat half a samosa and I'm working again.

He puts his hands over his face. The YOUNGER SISTER
returns.

Where is she now? One of you should have accompanied her –
that's what you're here for! Eating my food, taking up space,
the heating on all day. I have to spend my life out there on
the roads but my honour is here, in my house. And my
honour is your honour too.

The SISTERS *hang their heads.*

Don't take it the wrong way.

AMAR *enters with shopping bags.*

JAZ. You've been to the shops?

AMAR (*unwrapping them*). For flowers. It's spring. There should be flowers everywhere.

JAZ *watching her as she arranges them.*

How was your day?

JAZ. Choc-a-block.

The OLDER SISTER IN LAW *goes out.*

AMAR. Are you staying in tonight?

JAZ. I've got five cabs and four drivers. Tell a customer to wait ten minutes, he goes somewhere else. Money doesn't mint itself. This business is made on reputation.

AMAR (*she's heard it many times*). On reputation!

JAZ. A man has his work.

AMAR. And a woman hers! I'm not asking you to stay! Everything I need is here. Your sisters watch over me like I was a pot of gold. Food is prepared for me, the house gleams, the heating is up. Nothing to complain about. Everything is so peaceful. The way you want it. To live in peace.

JAZ. To live in peace a man must have peace of mind.

AMAR. You don't have peace of mind?

JAZ. I don't have it. No. I have nothing but worries.

AMAR. Then stop worrying. What do you want from me?

JAZ. You know very well.

AMAR. What? Say it.

JAZ (*reluctant to say what he really means*). You go out too much. How many times do I have to tell you? The street is not a place for a woman.

AMAR. Yes. You're quite right. A woman should be inside her house. That is where she will be safe and happy. (*Change of tone.*) Her house: if it is not a tomb, if the chairs become soft with sitting, if the sheets torn with use. But they aren't. Not in this house. Every night I find my bed newer and colder, stiff as if it has just come from the factory.

JAZ. So you admit it, I have reason to complain, to watch out.

AMAR. 'Reason to complain?' About what? 'Watch out?' Against what? I do nothing wrong. I obey you – in and out of our bed, I am submissive. I keep my suffering to myself now. It gets worse with every day – I don't complain about it to you any more. I put up with it. But you ask too much from me.

She picks up a flower and crushes it between her hands.

If I could suddenly turn into an old woman with a mouth like a bruised flower I would put up with it and smile and accept this life I'm living with you – but as it is now – just leave me to cope the best way I can.

JAZ. You carrying on like this – fucks me up! I don't understand what's going on inside your head. I do my best: anything you want I try and get it for you. I'm faithful, I don't gamble, I pay you compliments. I have my faults, I know, but I try. I try my best. Look, I want us to have a bit of peace between us, a nice life together, I can't rest with you like this. I want us to be at ease together.

He tries to put his arm around her but AMAR *pulls away.*

AMAR. I can't be at ease.

JAZ can't take much more. He swipes at the flower vase causing it to topple.

JAZ. Always the same. It's been five years now. You've got to forget it, like me, put it aside.

AMAR. But I'm not you, am I? Men have other things: their business, their sport, each other's company. The one thing that matters to a woman is her children: giving birth, rearing them.

JAZ. Not everyone can be the same. Bring one of your brother's children here, he has so many. I wouldn't mind, if it makes you happy.

AMAR. It's my own child I want, not someone else's. My arms would freeze just holding it.

JAZ (*exhausted by it all*). You know what's wrong with you Amar, there's a word for it. You're obsessed. Yes, obsessed.

You have only one thought, seeing only one thing, all the
time smashing your head against a concrete wall!

AMAR. Yes, concrete! When it should be flowers and sunshine.

JAZ. Life with you is constant anxiety. You keep going mental
on me at the smallest thing. It's no good. Can't you understand? Resign yourself to the facts. What is *is*. Get used to it.

AMAR. I didn't come to this country to 'resign myself'. When
they burn me and I'm dead, then I'll resign myself.

JAZ. OK. OK. So what do you want me to do?

AMAR. I want to drink water, but there is no glass. I want to
pick flowers but it is winter, I want to sew but there is no
thread.

JAZ. The fact is, you're not normal. That's the truth. You're not
normal and you want to destroy a man who tries to change
you.

AMAR. I no longer know who or what I am. I've never done
wrong by you. You're angry because I go out. I go out
because – because I can't stay in.

JAZ. I don't like the way fingers are pointing at me these days,
mouths whispering. You've been seen talking to strangers, to
people.

AMAR. Talking to people isn't a sin.

JAZ. But it can look like it.

The OLDER SISTER *enters with cutlery and goes over to a
drawer into which she places each piece of cutlery into its
right section.*

JAZ. I want the front door and the back doors kept shut, the
curtains closed and everyone inside.

The YOUNGER SISTER *enters and closes curtains. She now
picks up spilt flowers and rights the jug.* AMAR *knocks it
over again.*

JAZ (*under his breath to* AMAR *as he holds her tight by the
arm*). Things have got to change. From now on when people
talk to you, you keep your eyes down and your mouth shut.
Remember all the time: you're a married woman.

AMAR. Married!

JAZ. And that a family has its good name and every one in it is responsible for the honour of that name. It is in our blood!

He bangs the table.

Yes, even if it is thin and dark, our good name runs in our blood. (*Lowering voice.*) I'm sorry, but that's a fact.

The OLDER SISTER *leaves.*

Whether you like it or not.

AMAR *throws* JAZ *a look.*

JAZ (*catching her glance*). That look you're giving me, I shouldn't be saying 'sorry'. I should be forcing you to do as you're told.

AMAR *laughs.*

Locking you in. I'm your husband. I give the orders.

The two SISTERS *appear in doorway.*

AMAR. Don't say any more to me, please.

JAZ. Let's eat. Did you hear me?

The TWO SISTERS *leave.*

AMAR (*gently*). You eat with your sisters. I'm not hungry.

JAZ (*exiting*). Do what you want.

AMAR *picks up the flowers and plucks the petals from them.*

AMAR. Do what I want, do what I want. I want to carry a child. The dreaming moon gives me dead petals. In my flesh two warm springs, fountains of warm milk, racing like two fine horses, my pulse branching into anguished thudding wildness. Blind breasts beneath my dress, doves without eyes, doves without whiteness. The pain of imprisoned blood nailing wasps into the back of my neck.

She draws back the curtain and stares out.

But my love, my child, you must come. You must surely come my child, my love, my son. As sea bears salt, as the earth bears fruit. As a woman's womb swells tenderly to hold a child. As a cloud carries sweet rain, you must come!

She raps on the window and runs to the door and opens it.

AMAR (*calling*). Darshna! Darshna! Don't run away!

DARSHNA *enters with a baby in a buggy.*

Why are you running past my house?

DARSHNA. I always do when I have the baby with me. Because you always cry!

AMAR. You're right. (*Picking up the baby.*) I always cry. I can't help it.

DARSHNA. It upsets me that you're so envious, that's why I hurry by.

AMAR. I'm not envious – I'm deprived, that's what I feel. Deprived.

DARSHNA. It's no good going on and on about it, Amar. No good.

AMAR. I can't help it. I see you and the other women blossoming and here I am stunted and useless.

DARSHNA. Look, you have other things. You could be happy.

AMAR. A Punjabi girl who doesn't produce sons – she is as useless as a handful of husks. Empty and useless. Take him away – my shadow might fall on him.

DARSHNA *reaches for her baby.*

DARSHNA. Why do you say these things?.

AMAR. Because it's true. I'm cursed without a child of my own. I cry in here. (*Punching her stomach.*) I'm hurt and humiliated by my condition. Watching the prams pushing by, the buds breaking in the trees in the park, the birds so busy with their nests cheep cheep cheep up there. (*The roof.*) I can't stand to hear it any more. Even the dogs and cats are bursting with life. It seems as if nature is deliberately rising up around me to show me its young drowsing at their mother's side so contentedly while I feel nothing but hammer blows (*Touching her breasts.*) here and here where my baby's sweet mouth should be!

DARSHNA. Amar!

AMAR. You women with children, you can't imagine what it's like for us without. You 'wish I wouldn't talk like this'. It shows you're ignorant of the pain inside me, like a fish swimming in water, that has no idea what thirst is.

DARSHNA. I'm not going to bother to repeat what I'm always telling you.

AMAR. No, there's no point. Because what you don't understand is that it doesn't get better. I want it more and more and the longer it goes on the less hope there is.

DARSHNA. Don't say that.

AMAR. There is so little woman left in me I'll end up thinking I'm my own son. D'you know I often slip out at night to feed the guard dogs Jaz has tied up at the back. In the dark my footsteps sound to me like a man walking.

DARSHNA. Everyone has got a purpose in life.

AMAR. In spite of everything he still goes on wanting me. You see the life I'm leading.

DARSHNA. What about his sisters?

AMAR. I'll be dust and ashes before I speak to those two.

DARSHNA. And Jaswant?

AMAR. It's three against one.

DARSHNA. What are they up to?

AMAR. They imagine things. They've got dirty minds – like all people with a guilty conscience. They think I might go off with another man. They don't understand that even if I wanted to, in my family honour has always come FIRST. They are stones. Stones in my way. What they don't realise is that if I wished to I could be a hurricane and in one torrent sweep them away.

The YOUNGER SISTER IN LAW *enters and takes the vase of flowers away.*

DARSHNA. Anyway I'm sure Jaswant still loves you.

AMAR. He gives me food and shelter.

DARSHNA. I know it's difficult for you, Amar, but remember Bibi Nanaki's suffering.

AMAR (*looking at baby*). He's awake.

DARSHNA. Any minute he'll start crying.

AMAR. He has your eyes, did you know? Have you looked at them closely? (*She weeps.*) The same eyes as you.

AMAR *pushes the buggy gently towards the door.*
DARSHNA *leaves in sad silence. As* AMAR *is about to close the door* BACHAN *steps into the doorway.*

BACHAN (*whispering*). I waited for her to leave. My mother says, yes, she'll see you straight away.

AMAR. Thank you. Tell her, I'll come.

AMAR *goes to her bag to give the girl money.* ARVIND *steps in.*

BACHAN (*covering*). As I said, I'll bring the jacket later if that's all right with you.

AMAR. As you like.

BACHAN *leaves.*

ARVIND. Jaz at home?

AMAR. He's here. Eating. Sit down.

ARVIND (*no*). I'm OK.

AMAR (*calling*). Jaswant!

JAZ (*offstage*). In a minute. I'm just finishing.

ARVIND. I've called to say goodbye.

AMAR (*shaken, but controlling it*). Are you going back?

ARVIND. My father wants me back. To work with my brothers.

AMAR. Your father, he must be getting old now.

ARVIND Pretty old.

Pause.

AMAR. You're doing the right thing, moving back. Yes, I'm sure it's right.

ARVIND. It's not going to be that much different for me.

AMAR. I'd like to go away. Far away.

ARVIND. Yea? I think it's all much the same wherever you go. Business is business.

AMAR. For men, I agree. But women are different. They feel more. You men just get on with what you're doing. For you sun is sun and rain is rain. But me, I even notice which way the rain slants.

ARVIND *laughs*.

Women see differently. It's true.

ARVIND. I won't argue with that.

AMAR. Arvind.

ARVIND. Yes?

AMAR. Why are you going away? Everyone here likes you.

ARVIND (*jesting to cover emotions*). So they should. I'm a genuine, warm and popular guy.

AMAR. You are. When I was a young girl in my village I slipped and fell and you lifted me up, do you remember? By the river. You washed the mud from my face and took me to my mother.

ARVIND *gives no indication one way or the other that he recollects this*.

You can't tell how things are going to work out.

ARVIND. Everything changes.

AMAR. Not everything. There are things bricked in behind walls that can't be changed because nobody can hear them, nobody knows about them.

ARVIND. That's the way it is.

The OLDER SISTER *appears and moves to window where she closes the curtain and stands watching silently.*

AMAR. But if suddenly they came out – the screaming would shake the world.

ARVIND. And what would be the good of that? Like they say back home: (*Quoting*) 'The water in the river, the flock in the fold, the moon in the sky and a man at his plough.'

AMAR. It's a shame we don't use the old sayings.

Distant sound of drumming from Bhangra instrument.

ARVIND. The drums.

JAZ (*entering, still wiping his hands he has just washed*). You're off then.

ARVIND. First thing.

JAZ. And we're all square? Anything outstanding?

ARVIND. Nothing outstanding. Everything is sorted.

JAZ (*to* AMAR). I bought his licence and cab from him. Good investment.

AMAR. Is it?

ARVIND (*to* AMAR). For you as well. It's been made over to your joint names: Amar Kaur and Jaswant Singh INC!

JAZ laughs.

AMAR. I had no idea.

JAZ (*with satisfaction*). Good investment. We're getting there.

ARVIND (*to* AMAR). Twelve cabs now. Your husband is piling it up nicely.

AMAR. Money breeds money.

The OLDER SISTER *exits.* ARVIND *puts out his hand to shake it with* JAZ.

JAZ. We'll have a drink together.

JAZ exits to get his coat.

ARVIND (*with a respectful traditional gesture to* AMAR). I wish this house all happiness.

They shake hands.

AMAR. Maybe the Gods will listen to you. Goodbye.

ARVIND *turns to go but checks and turns back as* AMAR *makes an imperceptible movement.*

ARVIND. Did you say something?

AMAR (*dramatic*). I said: 'Goodbye'.

ARVIND. Thank you.

The men go out. AMAR, *upset, staring at the hand she gave* ARVIND. *She looks around quickly for a scarf, puts it on her head and moves stealthily out of the house. The stage is almost dark. The* YOUNGER SISTER IN LAW *enters, switches on a light and looks around for* AMAR.

YOUNGER SISTER IN LAW (*calling softly*). Amar! Amar!

The OLDER SISTER IN LAW *enters, glances at her sister they both go to the door and call shrilly.*

BOTH SISTERS IN LAW. Amar! Amar! Amar!

Offstage sound of dogs barking. Bhangra music. The stage is dark.

Curtain. End of Act Two.

ACT THREE

Scene One

The MEDIUM'*s house.* MEDIUM *and* AMAR *enter.*

MEDIUM. So, you came here without your husband's permission?

AMAR. He doesn't believe in spells.

MEDIUM. But you do.

AMAR. I came here to get results. And I don't think you will cheat me.

MEDIUM (*pointing to screen covered with letters*). I have so many testimonials. Read. The last woman I saw she was English. Yes! They all come to me because I can do what the National Health can't do. She had been childless longer than you. She was very dry. Afterwards her belly softened beautifully and she gave birth to twins so quickly they came while she was having a bath in her own home. It happened so quickly. Two beautiful boys.

AMAR. And she is well?

MEDIUM. Well? She is ecstatic!

AMAR. Of course she is. It's more natural. I wouldn't care where I had my baby. At home, in the street, in the hospital, even alone. I wouldn't care. I would know what to do, just like an animal knows what to do, it doesn't have to read a book on the subject. It picks up its young and licks it clean, I'd wash my baby and hold it close and when it opened its little mouth guide it my milk. And we'd lie softly together, me, gazing at its beautiful head and it sucking to the sound of milky streams filling my breasts, until we're both satisfied and he'll pull his pretty head away and there will be white drops of milk on my breast. Giving birth is so natural, so beautiful.

MEDIUM. You will have a child now, because I can see it. Believe me.

42

AMAR. I will have a child because I've got to have one. Because without one I can't make sense of myself, of anything. Sometimes . . . a wave of anger sweeps through me and everything seems meaningless. The people around me, in the street, the traffic, even the pavements seem made of cloth – thin cloth and I ask myself: Why have they been put here, what for?'

MEDIUM. Some would say: It is natural for a married woman such as yourself to want children. But if they don't come – why this mad desire for them? Are there not enough children in the world? What is it that is so urgent, so essential? What is it you think you can offer that is so special? What future is it you are dreaming and promising for it?

AMAR. The future doesn't concern me, It's NOW that matters. I'm living now.

MEDIUM. Is that really so?

AMAR. You're old. You see everything like it has already happened, a book already written. For me nothing yet has happened. I can think only of my yearning. I want to hold my baby in my arms and then I'll be able to sleep at nights.

The MEDIUM *makes a snorting disbelieving sound.*

AMAR. I'm going to tell you something and it may shock you. Even if I knew for certain that one day my son would torment me, hate me, drag me through the streets by my hair – still I would welcome his birth with pleasure, with joy! Why? Because it is much better to weep over a living man who stabs you with a knife than to weep over this ghost that sits in my heart pressing harder, weighing heavier year after year.

MEDIUM. My dear you are too emotional, too young to take advice now. The time will come, the time will come. But meanwhile try to take refuge in your husband's love.

AMAR. That's the worst of it.

MEDIUM. Your husband, he's a good man.

AMAR (*standing*). Yes. He is good. He's good. So what? I wish he was bad. But no, he goes to work, sees to his business, counts his money every night, and afterwards he lies on me in bed and does his duty but his body feels as cold as a corpse when it should be setting me on fire – bringing me life

MEDIUM. My dear –

AMAR. It's not sex. I'm not that kind of woman. But I do know it takes a man and a woman together to make children. If only I could have one by myself!

MEDIUM. Your husband, he is suffering too, don't forget.

AMAR. No. He is not suffering. He doesn't want children.

MEDIUM. Your husband doesn't want children? Are you certain?

AMAR. I see it in his eyes. And since he doesn't want them he makes sure he doesn't give them to me. I don't love him. I don't love him. But he is all I have. My only hope.

MEDIUM. I think you'd better be getting home – your time is up now. Wear this and this is the prayer.

AMAR. How often do I say the prayer?

She takes money from her bag and places it on MEDIUM's *table.*

MEDIUM. Before you sleep and after you wake. Your time is up now. (*Returning the money, seeing* AMAR *out.*) No, no, when you know you are pregnant send whatever gift you can afford.

On this JAZ *enters. He is furious. The money is still in the* MEDIUM's *hand.*

JAZ. So this is where you go. We've been searching everywhere.

AMAR. Now you've found me.

JAZ. What have you been saying, shouting your mouth off about again? Where else have you been with your noise and raving?

AMAR. If I could shout I would. I'd shout and scream loud enough to make the dead come to life to protest my innocence! I have done nothing! I am blameless.

JAZ. Not that again. I'm not having it any more. I'm being made a fool of. I'm an ordinary person – I can't keep up with your games.

AMAR. I've done nothing!

JAZ. You deceive me, you confuse me, I can't deal with it any more. You're a liar, that's what you are! A cunning liar!

AMAR Jaz!

JAZ. I don't want to hear another word out of you.

MEDIUM. Your wife: she has done nothing wrong.

JAZ. She's been wrong since the day I married her. Looking daggers at me, watching me while I sleep, her eyes wide open, sighing, those evil sighs into my pillows.

AMAR. Shut up!

JAZ. I've had enough. Only a saint could live with a wife who tries to reach into your heart with her jabbing fingers and wanders the streets at night looking, looking for what? Spoiling my reputation. The streets are full of men on the make. You don't go out on the streets to pick flowers. (*His face so close to* AMAR'*s his saliva sprays on her face*) Do you!

AMAR (*wiping his spit from her face*). I'm not listening to you. Not listening to a word. You and your family imagine you are the only ones with a reputation. But I'll tell you something: MY family has never had anything to hide.

She grabs him by the shoulders.

Come! Come closer and tell me if you can find a smell that is not yours. Smell my clothes, my hair. Can you find anything that is not from your body, any smell from another man? You can strip me naked and stand me in front of all the people and spit on me. I'm your wife, you can do what you like with me – but I warn you, don't you dare put another man's name between my legs.

JAZ. I don't have to, you're doing a fantastic job of it for yourself! The way you're carrying on, people are starting to point at you and talk!

AMAR *laughs at this.*

JAZ. I enter the office, everybody goes quiet. I order a drink, I get a funny look. My regular customers, they're not friendly like they used to be with me. They're not easy. There's a look in their eye. Why? You tell me why?

AMAR. I don't know. It rains on the pavements. I don't blame the pavements.

JAZ. And I don't know what a woman is looking for out of her house at all hours.

AMAR *clasps and clings on to him.*

AMAR (*emotional*). I'm looking for you! You! That's who I'm looking for day and night, looking, looking . . . without anywhere to shelter, to rest. Jaz it's you, your blood and your help I yearn for.

JAZ (*disengaging*). You – you keep away from me!

AMAR. Don't push me away! Yearn with me!

JAZ. Stop that!

AMAR. Look at my eyes. Don't you see how lonely I am*?* As if the moon was searching for itself in the skies. Look at me!

She looks at him. JAZ looks at her. He pushes her away roughly. She manages to cling. He pushes again.

JAZ. Leave me alone. Once and for all.

MEDIUM (*to* JAZ).Beta, please!

AMAR *falls to the ground. She takes time to recover herself. Something inside her has changed.*

AMAR (*loudly*). Wherever I searched for flowers I found weeds.

MEDIUM. Dear God!

AMAR (*screaming*). I curse my father, I curse my father who gave me his blood, the blood that could father a hundred sons. I curse my blood, my blood that hammers in me to make those sons.

JAZ. I told you to be quiet!

MEDIUM. Hush, keep your voices down, people will hear!

AMAR. I don't care what they hear. My voice can be free of caring. I'm falling into darkness. Falling, falling. Let at least one thing come out of my body to fill the air.

MEDIUM. Madam, I have other clients outside, they are waiting.

AMAR. Waiting! Who has been waiting longer than me? I know about waiting.

JAZ. Can't you be silent!

AMAR. I can be silent. Of course I can. Don't worry. I will be silent all right.

JAZ. OK. Let's go. Now!

AMAR. I'm coming – I can fool my head into doing anything. It's my body I can't cheat, my damn woman's body. All of you are right, there is no point in trying to fight back a river with my hands. That's it. It's over. I'll shut up. It's my fate, my kismet.

She leaves.

Scene Two

In the park. A Festival/Fair again. A song and dance number. The song is suggestive, lewd in English and Punjabi.

The OLD WOMAN *(from Act One in the park) is sitting on a bench by a tiny tent advertising 'Your Future Foreseen' clapping her hands to the music. Sitting alongside her a* YOUNG GIRL. *Behind them a large tent.*

OLD WOMAN. You going in there? (*The tent.*)

The YOUNG GIRL *nods shyly.*

You know what I read? There was a new guru last year. He was said to have magical powers, especially in female matters. Women came to him to cure their intimate troubles. He was had up for molesting and doing disgusting things to the women under false pretences. Two years in prison. It's true.

YOUNG GIRL. So what are you in the queue for?

OLD WOMAN. Every year more and more single men are hanging around behind these tents. But you don't see them going in. Only the young girls. Last year there was a fight.

TWO WOMEN *come out of the tent and exit. The* YOUNG GIRL *prepares to go in.*

Two men killed each other over a married woman. Always something happening on these festive occasions. People get stirred up.

The YOUNG GIRL *goes into he tent. The* OLD WOMAN
exits. DARSHNA *enters with a* GIRL (FIRST GIRL) *eating
sweets from a paper cone.*

FIRST GIRL (*pointing*). Wonder what she's doing here?

DARSHNA Who?

FIRST GIRL. Amar. I'm sure it was her just gone behind the
tent.

DARSHNA (*looking, but can't see her*). She's hasn't been out of
her chair for a the past month. Doesn't answer when you talk
to her. Scary. Something going on in her head. Something
bad. You can feel it.

FIRST GIRL. There's Miti. (*She waves.*) Look at her. So garish
in that colour. Candy pink! (*Waves and smiles.*) Last year she
went to have her fortune told and some young lads got hold
of her behind the stalls and groped her breasts!

DARSHNA. You hear nothing but dirty talk these days. And so
much drinking. They go wild, The club is stacked up with
crates for the bash the men are having later on. Stacked to the
ceiling. Hordes of them are coming from all over.

FIRST GIRL I'm not complaining! We could do with some
turbans around here.

They laugh and exit. From inside we hear AMAR, *and*
CHORUS *of* WOMEN *intoning.*

AMAR. Make my rose flower, don't leave me in the shade to
wither.

CHORUS. Let the pink rose bloom.

AMAR. Let the earth's dark flame burn.

CHORUS. Make this rose to flower, Don't leave it in the shade
to wither, make the rose to flower.

AMAR. Make me the miracle I seek, bring the Morning back to
my life, even though it bears a thousand thorns, let the rose
grow, let the petals of my heart open to the sun.

CHORUS. Take pity on this woman, make her rose to flower.

The Bhangra group now appear and perform.

Pretty wife come to celebrate
But leave off your heavy clothes
How pale the sorrowful wife,
Oh she sighs, so sadly.
She'll be a rose when her man
Undoes her clothing,
Take off your heavy clothes
Pretty wife . . .

Take the weight of my heavy body
Oh how she glows,
Oh how she sways,
Seven times she moaned,
Nine times she rose and fifteen times the rose turned
    to orange and the orange turned to red.
She bends like a reed,
She fades like a flower,
Pretty, pretty wife,
Leave off your heavy clothes.

The Bhangra group move off almost knocking over the OLD
WOMAN *who enters to sit outside the tent again. She shouts
to the Bhangra group to watch where they are going.*

AMAR *comes out of the large tent.*

OLD WOMAN. It's you! You've been in there? (*The tent.*)

AMAR *nods.*

OLD WOMAN. Surely you don't believe in that nonsense?

AMAR. I don't know.

OLD WOMAN. Your husband, what about him?

AMAR (*points, tired*). He's over there, drinking. Oh God!

OLD WOMAN (*looking closely at* AMAR). Less of the God.
    Listen to me. I couldn't tell you anything before. But I can
    tell you now.

AMAR (*without spirit*). What, what can you tell me that I don't
    already know?

JAZ *appears, sees the two women talking and hides behind
placards.*

OLD WOMAN. Something that can't be kept from you any longer. Everyone knows. They don't even put their hands before their mouths as they say it. It's your husband's fault. Do you understand? Your husband is to blame. They can cut off both my hands if I tell a lie. It's a known fact: not his father, his grandfather, not his great grandfather, none of them were manly men. Not six inches between them. Heaven and earth had to be moved for them to make a son. In that family the men are made of spit. The opposite of your people, people with good, rich blood. You have so many brothers and cousins multiplying themselves. Your husband's family, men are a rarity. You have been used to bring fruit to a dead tree. This my dear is your curse.

AMAR. A spray of poison over the rose. It will never open. It might as well never have bloomed.

OLD WOMAN. But why? You've got feet, you can walk out on him.

AMAR. Walk out.

OLD WOMAN. I have one son, a bachelor at home, still not married, a little shy but with good strong blood. All my sons have good blood, plenty of children. And not all by their wives! If you go into his bed you will find it smells of babies.

AMAR (horrified). I couldn't. I couldn't.

OLD WOMAN (misunderstanding). You don't have to worry what people will say. My sons will protect you from insults. We're a strong family.

AMAR. Wagging tongues, that is not the problem. I don't care what other people think. It's not that.

OLD WOMAN. Your bed of ashes will turn into a river of milk for your children in my son's arms. I'm telling you.

AMAR. Do you imagine I could ever search for another man, sleep with another man?

OLD WOMAN. And why not? These are modern times!

AMAR. Water can't flow backwards, the moon can't shine at noon. I have my honour.

OLD WOMAN. Your honour!

50

AMAR. Slut! Get out of my sight!

OLD WOMAN. I took pity on you. I was trying to help you.

AMAR. Did you really think I could turn to another man, go begging like a slave for what is mine by right? I'm not here looking for another man.

OLD WOMAN. When you're dying of thirst you don't become choosy about the quality of the jug that holds your drink.

AMAR. I'm like a parched desert in need of a flood. What you're offering me is a tiny glass of tap water. My pain is beyond that kind of comfort.

OLD WOMAN (*angry*). Then carry on, if that's what you prefer, carry on in your barren desert of thorns and thistles.

AMAR. Barren, yes, that's right. 'Banj!' You don't have to press the word into my ears, enjoy taunting me with it. 'Barren!' I've been hiding from that word from the first month since I got married. This is the first time it's been said to my face. Barren! The first time I've realised it's true. Thank you.

OLD WOMAN. I should feel pity for you. But I don't. I don't feel it at all. I'll find another woman for my son. A normal woman.

She exits. Sound of Bhangra band again. JAZ *appears from his hiding place and circles* AMAR.

AMAR. Did you hear it all?

JAZ. Most of it.

AMAR. You were spying on me.

JAZ. If you like.

AMAR. It doesn't matter what I like, does it? Let's go and listen to the singers.

JAZ. It's time I had my say.

AMAR. Speak!

JAZ. It's time.

AMAR. Then open your mouth and speak. Tell me what it is you want to complain about.

JAZ. About – about the bitterness in my throat.

AMAR. Only your throat! I have it in my bones.

JAZ. I can't go on any more with you. With your scenes, with your rantings to strangers, your imagined grievances, the stuff you make up out of thin air.

AMAR (*violent*). Imaginings, you call it, stuff I make up!

JAZ. Things between us that haven't happened. Things that neither of us can control.

AMAR. Go on! Go on! Don't stop now!

JAZ. Things I don't care about, that I'm not interested in. Do you understand? Things that don't matter (*Claps his hand to illustrate.*) that much to me.

AMAR. You don't care.

JAZ. I'm telling you honestly. I'm not bothered. All that matters to me is what I can hold in my hands. What I can see with my eyes. I can't spend my life grieving for something that does not exist!

AMAR lets out a long spine chilling cry. And then she collapses, holding her head.

AMAR (*on her knees*). So that's it. That's it. I wanted to hear it from your own mouth. The truth. It's been hiding unspoken all this time a tiny thing, but how enormous it is now it is uttered, how loud it screams. For the first time I realise what it is you're saying. YOU DON'T CARE!

She cries.

JAZ (*coming close to her*). We have to tell ourselves it was meant to be, it's our fate! Listen to me –

He puts his arms round her to raise her up.

Listen to me! It's not such a tragedy. Many women would be happy to live your life. Without children life is simpler, not so many problems. I am happy without them. We are not to blame.

AMAR (*cold*). So what did you want me for?

JAZ. For you. Yourself.

AMAR. Yes, that's it. That's what YOU wanted. A house, a quiet life, a good business and a woman. That's true, isn't it? that's all you wanted.

JAZ. Yea. Same as other people.

AMAR. And nothing else. What about your son?

JAZ (*ferocious*). Didn't you hear me? I DON'T CARE! You keep on and on about it. Do I have to shout it into your ear to get it into your head once and for all, to get through to you: I DON'T CARE! Now can we have some peace on the subject once and for all?

He tries to push her away but she clings to him.

AMAR. You never yearned for a son?

JAZ. No. Never.

AMAR. And I have no hope of one?

JAZ No.

AMAR. Nor you.

JAZ. Nor me either. Accept it.

AMAR. Barren.

Offstage sound of PEOPLE *laughing, festive music.*

JAZ. Accept it Amar. Reconcile. Let me and you try and live in peace together, without fighting, without aggravation. Come on, it'll be nice. Touch me, just touch me.

AMAR. What are you after?

JAZ. You Amar, you're still a very beautiful woman, beautiful, do you know that, I want you. (*Looking round.*) I yearn for you.

AMAR. You want me like the way you want a piece of fresh killed chicken for your supper.

JAZ. Touch me. Touch me like this. Like this.

AMAR. Never. Never.

AMAR *cries out and clutches* JAZ *by the throat. He falls back. She sustains the pressure on his neck until she kills him.*

AMAR. Childless. Childless. But I know it for certain. And
I can face it. Alone. Now I can sleep without waking and
fearing to know if my blood is making new blood inside me.
Now I can rest. My body will be barren forever. An end to
longing. An end to hoping. (*Bitter.*) I will be at peace. What
more do you want to know? Don't come near me. For I have
killed my son! I have killed my own child. It's finished.

PEOPLE *gather upstage in festive clothes, dancing and
singing. AMAR is very still as they continue with the singing.*

Curtain.

End.

A YEARNING
Ruth Carter

A transposition of *Yerma* into the Punjabi community of Britain, *A Yearning* gives Lorca's classic a vibrant twist as Spanish metaphors find their counterpart in Punjabi earthiness.

Amar, a bride from India, marries Jaz, a Glaswegian Punjabi, and comes to live in Birmingham. She yearns for a child to fill her empty lap, but Jaz, owner of a mini-cab firm, is too preoccupied with his business to concern himself with her loneliness and longing.

A Yearning focuses on the plight of a woman married into a society where her real worth is measured by her ability to have children. Faced with her failure to conceive, the community, at first nurturing, becomes increasingly stifling.

A Yearning was co-produced by the Tamasha Theatre Company with the Birmingham Rep in 1995, touring the UK and playing at the Lyric Theatre, Hammersmith. 'An intelligent, thought provoking production, opening a surprisingly accurate window into the aims and aspirations of the Punjabi community in our city.'
Birmingham Weekly Observer

'A highly successful company of national importance'
Arts Council of England

PLAYS   £6.99

ISBN 1-85459-450-8

9 781854 594501

Cover: Archie Panjabi and Sudha Bhuchar,
Photo: Sue Mayes

TAMASHA PLAYS

HOUSE
OF THE SUN

Sudha Bhuchar and
Kristine Landon-Smith

adapted from the novel
by Meira Chand

tamasha [21]

Tamasha is 21 years old in 2010. The product of a unique partnership between director Kristine Landon-Smith and actor/playwright Sudha Bhuchar. Tamasha has inspired and challenged audiences since 1989, developing a vast body of work from an Asian cultural context. Major productions include their debut *Untouchable*, the Tamasha-commissioned *East is East* and *Ghostdancing*, and the recently acclaimed *Wuthering Heights*. Alongside this, Tamasha's Developing Artists programme discovers and supports new Asian artists of all disciplines.

Other titles available from Tamasha in your library include:

Untouchable (1989)
House of the Sun (1991)
Women of the Dust (1992)
A Shaft of Sunlight (1994)
A Tainted Dawn (1997)
Fourteen Songs, Two Weddings and a Funeral (1998/2001)
Ghostdancing (2001)
Strictly Dandia (2003)
Wuthering Heights (2009)

For further information about the company and its plays, please go to: www.tamasha.org.uk